MGISCRE
CREATE+MGIS

create.mgis.start

Mgiscre.ask.davidgomadza.start.start.start

David Gomadza

President Tomorrow's World Order

Yahweh's Representative on Earth

www.twofuture.world

Copyright © 2024 David Gomadza

All rights reserved.

PAPERBACK ISBN: 9798338957608

DEDICATION

A Better World

TABLE OF CONTENTS

MGISCRE SYSTEMS NETWORK AND CODES 1

NTL CODE 37

COBOL 38

    LETS IMPROVE MGISCRE 39

MGISCRE NETWORK 40

DEFINITIONS AND DESCRIPTION OF EACH NETWORK ENTITY 43

SYSTEM FUNCTIONS AND PERIPHERIES 52

RECAP FROM MGISCRE BY DAVID GOMADZA 52

MGISCRE 52

ACKNOWLEDGMENTS

visit www.twofuture.world

signed david gomadza
ask.davidgomadzaauthorised.licensed.checkya.askya.ya

11 September 2024 16.00PM
Scotland
00447719210295
davidgomadza@hotmail.com
info@twofuture.world

WARNING WARNING

YOU NEED MINIMUM LONGAGO OF 28SECONDS [12].START

MGISCRE SYSTEMS NETWORK AND CODES

Transferring cobol to mgiscre I have developed this mgiscre software to make sure that I can be advanced in everything and its something you have never seen as the body created antidots instead but became human meaning reduced mgis in a human that can die which is the opposite but a clever way to say I am human hence mgis shifted down to operations on earth but made mgiscre the best software on earth because i assigned create for defense and mgis for the operations hence the confusion because mgis is for the presidential so now we can turn mgiscre to presidential by a simple command mgiscre.ask.davidgomadza.start.turnoperationsintopresidential[president oftomorrowsworldorderdavidgomadza].start[forever^{1600}]

mgiscre.ask.davidgomadza.start.reboot.start[forever^{1600}deaddead]

Mgiscre is the latest software on the market by me[davidgomadza] and is one of the most robust software on earth but without the softness of heaven because this attacks enemies because the others to keep marketable have developed a series of invaders that blocks competition from others and as such field in their no braines every 2 minutes to kill and invade any software on the market to kill and invade any software but it can also be a case of one constantly attacking with invaders that sad as we speak now calculate his long ago as no human can use mgiscre even more now as we will use compounding checks of long ago we can also ask who else can help to find out who other experts sell what you can then go now we have sold items
mgiscre.ask.davidgomadza.start.leaveall2000seatsopen.start[forever^{1600}]

Starting

Presidentialandbusinessdeals.start[everything]

If we ask what this can be used for here is a list from its manuals

1] interconnections
2] meetings
3] conferences
4] startuppackages
5] scheduling
6] assortedmeetings
7] stocktrading
8] modullationinreality
9] presidentialspooning
10] presidentialappointments
11] presidentialannouncements
12] presidentialflyerer
13] presidentialhottopic
14] presidentialetc
15] operationsmanagingpeople
16] operatioonsinvoicing
17]operationstelephoningmodulation
18] askdot
19] askwhat
20] askdavidgomadza

mgiscre.ask.davidgomadza.start.removeallresiduesofeveryonewhoeverenteredforever^{1600}deaddead.start[forever^{1600}]
if I can now add new opportunities to make this unique first I will add a list of the obvious things that came with bot create and mgis to have mgiscre
mgiscre.ask.davidgomadza.startcleanasyougo.start[forever^{1600}]
mgiscre.ask.davidgomadza.start.removeallresidueofeveryonewhoeverenteredforever^{1600}deaddead.start[forever^{1600}][forever^{1610}forever^{1620}]
starting

checkmanualsstarting
startingmanuals
manualsstarting
startingcreate[defense]
startingmgis[presidentialoperationsetc]
startingmgiscre[both]
startingmanuals[both]
manualsstrtaing
startingmanuals
startingboth
startingmgiscre
mgiscrestarting
startingmgiscre
mgiscrestarting
runmgiscre
mgiscrerun
runmgiscre
actmgiscre
askmgiscre
mgiscreact
mgiscreask
mgiscrereply
mgiscreask
askmgiscre
replymgiscre
askagainmgiscre
sayagainmgiscre
talkmgiscre
askmgiscre
inquiremgiscre
informmgiscre
abundantmgiscre
askagainmgiscre
ifnotyouthenwho
ifyouthenwhen

ifnotnowthenwhen
ifnotusthenwho
ifnotusthenwho
ificanthenwhen
ifnotmethenwho
ifnotthenwho
ifnotmethenwho
ifnotusthenwho
ifnotmethenwho
whocanandwhy
ifnotmethenwho
ifnotwhothenwhen
icanandwhen
ificantthenwho
ificantthenwho
ificanthenwhen
ificantthenwho
ificanthenwhen
ificanthenwithwhat
icanandhow
icanandwhen
icanandwithwhat
icanwithwho
icanandwhen
icanthenwhen
icanthenwithwhom
ificanthenwhen
ificanthenwhenandhow
ificanthenwithwhatandhow
ificanthenhow
ificanwithwho
ificanthenwhen
ificanthenhow
ificanthenhowandwhen
ificanwithwhat

ificanthenwithwhat
ifwecanthenhow
ifwecanthenhowandwhen
ifweaskthenwho
whocanandwhy
whoandwhy
ifnotusthenwho
ifnotyouthenwho
ifnotthemthenwho
ifnotusthenwho
ifnotusthenwho
ifnotusthenwho
whatcanbe
whatcouldbe
whathasbeen
whatistobe
whatcanbe
whatwas
whatcanbe
whatcouldbe
whatwas
whatwill
whatcan
whatcouldbe
whatshouldbe
whatwas
whatcan
whatcanbe
whatcouldbe
whatwas
whatis
whatistobe
whatcanbe
whatcouldbe

mgiscre.ask.davidgomadza.start.hailhailhailodavidgomadzafirstmgiscreeveronearth.startx8.initialise.now.save.start.start[forever^{1600}]

BRAIN
starting
checkmanualsstarting
startingmanuals
manualsstarting
startingcreate[defense]
startingmgis[presidentialoperationsetc]
startingmgiscre[both]
startingmanuals[both]
manualsstrtaing
startingmanuals
startingboth
startingmgiscre
mgiscrestarting
startingmgiscre
mgiscrestarting
runmgiscre
mgiscrerun
runmgiscre
actmgiscre
askmgiscre
mgiscreact
mgiscreask
mgiscrereply
mgiscreask
askmgiscre
replymgiscre
askagainmgiscre
sayagainmgiscre
talkmgiscre
askmgiscre
inquiremgiscre

informmgiscre
abundantmgiscre
askagainmgiscre
ifnotyouthenwho
ifyouthenwhen
ifnotnowthenwhen
ifnotusthenwho
ifnotusthenwho
ificanthenwhen
ifnotmethenwho
ifnotthenwho
ifnotmethenwho
ifnotusthenwho
ifnotmethenwho
whocanandwhy
ifnotmethenwho
ifnotwhothenwhen
icanandwhen
ificantthenwho
ificantthenwho
ificanthenwhen
ificantthenwho
ificanthenwhen
ificanthenwithwhat
icanandhow
icanandwhen
icanandwithwhat
icanwithwho
icanandwhen
icanthenwhen
icanthenwithwhom
ificanthenwhen
ificanthenwhenandhow
ificanthenwithwhatandhow
ificanthenhow

ificanwithwho
ificanthenwhen
ificanthenhow
ificanthenhowandwhen
ificanwithwhat
ificanthenwithwhat
ifwecanthenhow
ifwecanthenhowandwhen
ifweaskthenwho
whocanandwhy
whoandwhy
ifnotusthenwho
ifnotyouthenwho
ifnotthemthenwho
ifnotusthenwho
ifnotusthenwho
ifnotusthenwho
whatcanbe
whatcouldbe
whathasbeen
whatistobe
whatcanbe
whatwas
whatcanbe
whatcouldbe
whatwas
whatwill
whatcan
whatcouldbe
whatshouldbe
whatwas
whatcan
whatcanbe
whatcouldbe
whatwas

whatis
whatistobe
whatcanbe
whatcouldbe

RIGHT ARM
starting
checkmanualsstarting
startingmanuals
manualsstarting
startingcreate[defense]
startingmgis[presidentialoperationsetc]
startingmgiscre[both]
startingmanuals[both]
manualsstrtaing
startingmanuals
startingboth
startingmgiscre
mgiscrestarting
startingmgiscre
mgiscrestarting
runmgiscre
mgiscrerun
runmgiscre
actmgiscre
askmgiscre
mgiscreact
mgiscreask
mgiscrereply
mgiscreask
askmgiscre
replymgiscre
askagainmgiscre
sayagainmgiscre
talkmgiscre

askmgiscre
inquiremgiscre
informmgiscre
abundantmgiscre
askagainmgiscre
ifnotyouthenwho
ifyouthenwhen
ifnotnowthenwhen
ifnotusthenwho
ifnotusthenwho
ificanthenwhen
ifnotmethenwho
ifnotthenwho
ifnotmethenwho
ifnotusthenwho
ifnotmethenwho
whocanandwhy
ifnotmethenwho
ifnotwhothenwhen
icanandwhen
ificantthenwho
ificantthenwho
ificanthenwhen
ificantthenwho
ificanthenwhen
ificanthenwithwhat
icanandhow
icanandwhen
icanandwithwhat
icanwithwho
icanandwhen
icanthenwhen
icanthenwithwhom
ificanthenwhen
ificanthenwhenandhow

ificanthenwithwhatandhow
ificanthenhow
ificanwithwho
ificanthenwhen
ificanthenhow
ificanthenhowandwhen
ificanwithwhat
ificanthenwithwhat
ifwecanthenhow
ifwecanthenhowandwhen
ifweaskthenwho
whocanandwhy
whoandwhy
ifnotusthenwho
ifnotyouthenwho
ifnotthemthenwho
ifnotusthenwho
ifnotusthenwho
ifnotusthenwho
whatcanbe
whatcouldbe
whathasbeen
whatistobe
whatcanbe
whatwas
whatcanbe
whatcouldbe
whatwas
whatwill
whatcan
whatcouldbe
whatshouldbe
whatwas
whatcan
whatcanbe

whatcouldbe
whatwas
whatis
whatistobe
whatcanbe
whatcouldbe

RIGHT LEG
starting
checkmanualsstarting
startingmanuals
manualsstarting
startingcreate[defense]
startingmgis[presidentialoperationsetc]
startingmgiscre[both]
startingmanuals[both]
manualsstrtaing
startingmanuals
startingboth
startingmgiscre
mgiscrestarting
startingmgiscre
mgiscrestarting
runmgiscre
mgiscrerun
runmgiscre
actmgiscre
askmgiscre
mgiscreact
mgiscreask
mgiscrereply
mgiscreask
askmgiscre
replymgiscre
askagainmgiscre

sayagainmgiscre
talkmgiscre
askmgiscre
inquiremgiscre
informmgiscre
abundantmgiscre
askagainmgiscre
ifnotyouthenwho
ifyouthenwhen
ifnotnowthenwhen
ifnotusthenwho
ifnotusthenwho
ificanthenwhen
ifnotmethenwho
ifnotthenwho
ifnotmethenwho
ifnotusthenwho
ifnotmethenwho
whocanandwhy
ifnotmethenwho
ifnotwhothenwhen
icanandwhen
ificantthenwho
ificantthenwho
ificanthenwhen
ificantthenwho
ificanthenwhen
ificanthenwithwhat
icanandhow
icanandwhen
icanandwithwhat
icanwithwho
icanandwhen
icanthenwhen
icanthenwithwhom

ificanthenwhen
ificanthenwhenandhow
ificanthenwithwhatandhow
ificanthenhow
ificanwithwho
ificanthenwhen
ificanthenhow
ificanthenhowandwhen
ificanwithwhat
ificanthenwithwhat
ifwecanthenhow
ifwecanthenhowandwhen
ifweaskthenwho
whocanandwhy
whoandwhy
ifnotusthenwho
ifnotyouthenwho
ifnotthemthenwho
ifnotusthenwho
ifnotusthenwho
ifnotusthenwho
whatcanbe
whatcouldbe
whathasbeen
whatistobe
whatcanbe
whatwas
whatcanbe
whatcouldbe
whatwas
whatwill
whatcan
whatcouldbe
whatshouldbe
whatwas

whatcan
whatcanbe
whatcouldbe
whatwas
whatis
whatistobe
whatcanbe
whatcouldbe

LEFT LEG
starting
checkmanualsstarting
startingmanuals
manualsstarting
startingcreate[defense]
startingmgis[presidentialoperationsetc]
startingmgiscre[both]
startingmanuals[both]
manualsstrtaing
startingmanuals
startingboth
startingmgiscre
mgiscrestarting
startingmgiscre
mgiscrestarting
runmgiscre
mgiscrerun
runmgiscre
actmgiscre
askmgiscre
mgiscreact
mgiscreask
mgiscrereply
mgiscreask
askmgiscre

replymgiscre
askagainmgiscre
sayagainmgiscre
talkmgiscre
askmgiscre
inquiremgiscre
informmgiscre
abundantmgiscre
askagainmgiscre
ifnotyouthenwho
ifyouthenwhen
ifnotnowthenwhen
ifnotusthenwho
ifnotusthenwho
ificanthenwhen
ifnotmethenwho
ifnotthenwho
ifnotmethenwho
ifnotusthenwho
ifnotmethenwho
whocanandwhy
ifnotmethenwho
ifnotwhothenwhen
icanandwhen
ificantthenwho
ificantthenwho
ificanthenwhen
ificantthenwho
ificanthenwhen
ificanthenwithwhat
icanandhow
icanandwhen
icanandwithwhat
icanwithwho
icanandwhen

icanthenwhen
icanthenwithwhom
ificanthenwhen
ificanthenwhenandhow
ificanthenwithwhatandhow
ificanthenhow
ificanwithwho
ificanthenwhen
ificanthenhow
ificanthenhowandwhen
ificanwithwhat
ificanthenwithwhat
ifwecanthenhow
ifwecanthenhowandwhen
ifweaskthenwho
whocanandwhy
whoandwhy
ifnotusthenwho
ifnotyouthenwho
ifnotthemthenwho
ifnotusthenwho
ifnotusthenwho
ifnotusthenwho
whatcanbe
whatcouldbe
whathasbeen
whatistobe
whatcanbe
whatwas
whatcanbe
whatcouldbe
whatwas
whatwill
whatcan
whatcouldbe

whatshouldbe
whatwas
whatcan
whatcanbe
whatcouldbe
whatwas
whatis
whatistobe
whatcanbe
whatcouldbe

LEFT ARM
starting
checkmanualsstarting
startingmanuals
manualsstarting
startingcreate[defense]
startingmgis[presidentialoperationsetc]
startingmgiscre[both]
startingmanuals[both]
manualsstrtaing
startingmanuals
startingboth
startingmgiscre
mgiscrestarting
startingmgiscre
mgiscrestarting
runmgiscre
mgiscrerun
runmgiscre
actmgiscre
askmgiscre
mgiscreact
mgiscreask
mgiscrereply

mgiscreask
askmgiscre
replymgiscre
askagainmgiscre
sayagainmgiscre
talkmgiscre
askmgiscre
inquiremgiscre
informmgiscre
abundantmgiscre
askagainmgiscre
ifnotyouthenwho
ifyouthenwhen
ifnotnowthenwhen
ifnotusthenwho
ifnotusthenwho
ificanthenwhen
ifnotmethenwho
ifnotthenwho
ifnotmethenwho
ifnotusthenwho
ifnotmethenwho
whocanandwhy
ifnotmethenwho
ifnotwhothenwhen
icanandwhen
ificantthenwho
ificantthenwho
ificanthenwhen
ificantthenwho
ificanthenwhen
ificanthenwithwhat
icanandhow
icanandwhen
icanandwithwhat

icanwithwho
icanandwhen
icanthenwhen
icanthenwithwhom
ificanthenwhen
ificanthenwhenandhow
ificanthenwithwhatandhow
ificanthenhow
ificanwithwho
ificanthenwhen
ificanthenhow
ificanthenhowandwhen
ificanwithwhat
ificanthenwithwhat
ifwecanthenhow
ifwecanthenhowandwhen
ifweaskthenwho
whocanandwhy
whoandwhy
ifnotusthenwho
ifnotyouthenwho
ifnotthemthenwho
ifnotusthenwho
ifnotusthenwho
ifnotusthenwho
whatcanbe
whatcouldbe
whathasbeen
whatistobe
whatcanbe
whatwas
whatcanbe
whatcouldbe
whatwas
whatwill

whatcan
whatcouldbe
whatshouldbe
whatwas
whatcan
whatcanbe
whatcouldbe
whatwas
whatis
whatistobe
whatcanbe
whatcouldbe

TOMB
starting
checkmanualsstarting
startingmanuals
manualsstarting
startingcreate[defense]
startingmgis[presidentialoperationsetc]
startingmgiscre[both]
startingmanuals[both]
manualsstrtaing
startingmanuals
startingboth
startingmgiscre
mgiscrestarting
startingmgiscre
mgiscrestarting
runmgiscre
mgiscrerun
runmgiscre
actmgiscre
askmgiscre
mgiscreact

mgiscreask
mgiscrereply
mgiscreask
askmgiscre
replymgiscre
askagainmgiscre
sayagainmgiscre
talkmgiscre
askmgiscre
inquiremgiscre
informmgiscre
abundantmgiscre
askagainmgiscre
ifnotyouthenwho
ifyouthenwhen
ifnotnowthenwhen
ifnotusthenwho
ifnotusthenwho
ificanthenwhen
ifnotmethenwho
ifnotthenwho
ifnotmethenwho
ifnotusthenwho
ifnotmethenwho
whocanandwhy
ifnotmethenwho
ifnotwhothenwhen
icanandwhen
ificantthenwho
ificantthenwho
ificanthenwhen
ificantthenwho
ificanthenwhen
ificanthenwithwhat
icanandhow

icanandwhen
icanandwithwhat
icanwithwho
icanandwhen
icanthenwhen
icanthenwithwhom
ificanthenwhen
ificanthenwhenandhow
ificanthenwithwhatandhow
ificanthenhow
ificanwithwho
ificanthenwhen
ificanthenhow
ificanthenhowandwhen
ificanwithwhat
ificanthenwithwhat
ifwecanthenhow
ifwecanthenhowandwhen
ifweaskthenwho
whocanandwhy
whoandwhy
ifnotusthenwho
ifnotyouthenwho
ifnotthemthenwho
ifnotusthenwho
ifnotusthenwho
ifnotusthenwho
whatcanbe
whatcouldbe
whathasbeen
whatistobe
whatcanbe
whatwas
whatcanbe
whatcouldbe

whatwas
whatwill
whatcan
whatcouldbe
whatshouldbe
whatwas
whatcan
whatcanbe
whatcouldbe
whatwas
whatis
whatistobe
whatcanbe
whatcouldbe

LIVER
starting
checkmanualsstarting
startingmanuals
manualsstarting
startingcreate[defense]
startingmgis[presidentialoperationsetc]
startingmgiscre[both]
startingmanuals[both]
manualsstrtaing
startingmanuals
startingboth
startingmgiscre
mgiscrestarting
startingmgiscre
mgiscrestarting
runmgiscre
mgiscrerun
runmgiscre
actmgiscre

askmgiscre
mgiscreact
mgiscreask
mgiscrereply
mgiscreask
askmgiscre
replymgiscre
askagainmgiscre
sayagainmgiscre
talkmgiscre
askmgiscre
inquiremgiscre
informmgiscre
abundantmgiscre
askagainmgiscre
ifnotyouthenwho
ifyouthenwhen
ifnotnowthenwhen
ifnotusthenwho
ifnotusthenwho
ificanthenwhen
ifnotmethenwho
ifnotthenwho
ifnotmethenwho
ifnotusthenwho
ifnotmethenwho
whocanandwhy
ifnotmethenwho
ifnotwhothenwhen
icanandwhen
ificantthenwho
ificantthenwho
ificanthenwhen
ificantthenwho
ificanthenwhen

ificanthenwithwhat
icanandhow
icanandwhen
icanandwithwhat
icanwithwho
icanandwhen
icanthenwhen
icanthenwithwhom
ificanthenwhen
ificanthenwhenandhow
ificanthenwithwhatandhow
ificanthenhow
ificanwithwho
ificanthenwhen
ificanthenhow
ificanthenhowandwhen
ificanwithwhat
ificanthenwithwhat
ifwecanthenhow
ifwecanthenhowandwhen
ifweaskthenwho
whocanandwhy
whoandwhy
ifnotusthenwho
ifnotyouthenwho
ifnotthemthenwho
ifnotusthenwho
ifnotusthenwho
ifnotusthenwho
whatcanbe
whatcouldbe
whathasbeen
whatistobe
whatcanbe
whatwas

whatcanbe
whatcouldbe
whatwas
whatwill
whatcan
whatcouldbe
whatshouldbe
whatwas
whatcan
whatcanbe
whatcouldbe
whatwas
whatis
whatistobe
whatcanbe
whatcouldbe

INSIDE RIGHT SPLEEN
starting
checkmanualsstarting
startingmanuals
manualsstarting
startingcreate[defense]
startingmgis[presidentialoperationsetc]
startingmgiscre[both]
startingmanuals[both]
manualsstrtaing
startingmanuals
startingboth
startingmgiscre
mgiscrestarting
startingmgiscre
mgiscrestarting
runmgiscre
mgiscrerun

runmgiscre
actmgiscre
askmgiscre
mgiscreact
mgiscreask
mgiscrereply
mgiscreask
askmgiscre
replymgiscre
askagainmgiscre
sayagainmgiscre
talkmgiscre
askmgiscre
inquiremgiscre
informmgiscre
abundantmgiscre
askagainmgiscre
ifnotyouthenwho
ifyouthenwhen
ifnotnowthenwhen
ifnotusthenwho
ifnotusthenwho
ificanthenwhen
ifnotmethenwho
ifnotthenwho
ifnotmethenwho
ifnotusthenwho
ifnotmethenwho
whocanandwhy
ifnotmethenwho
ifnotwhothenwhen
icanandwhen
ificantthenwho
ificantthenwho
ificanthenwhen

ificantthenwho
ificanthenwhen
ificanthenwithwhat
icanandhow
icanandwhen
icanandwithwhat
icanwithwho
icanandwhen
icanthenwhen
icanthenwithwhom
ificanthenwhen
ificanthenwhenandhow
ificanthenwithwhatandhow
ificanthenhow
ificanwithwho
ificanthenwhen
ificanthenhow
ificanthenhowandwhen
ificanwithwhat
ificanthenwithwhat
ifwecanthenhow
ifwecanthenhowandwhen
ifweaskthenwho
whocanandwhy
whoandwhy
ifnotusthenwho
ifnotyouthenwho
ifnotthemthenwho
ifnotusthenwho
ifnotusthenwho
ifnotusthenwho
whatcanbe
whatcouldbe
whathasbeen
whatistobe

whatcanbe
whatwas
whatcanbe
whatcouldbe
whatwas
whatwill
whatcan
whatcouldbe
whatshouldbe
whatwas
whatcan
whatcanbe
whatcouldbe
whatwas
whatis
whatistobe
whatcanbe
whatcouldbe

INSIDE LEFT SPLEEN
starting
checkmanualsstarting
startingmanuals
manualsstarting
startingcreate[defense]
startingmgis[presidentialoperationsetc]
startingmgiscre[both]
startingmanuals[both]
manualsstrtaing
startingmanuals
startingboth
startingmgiscre
mgiscrestarting
startingmgiscre
mgiscrestarting

runmgiscre
mgiscrerun
runmgiscre
actmgiscre
askmgiscre
mgiscreact
mgiscreask
mgiscrereply
mgiscreask
askmgiscre
replymgiscre
askagainmgiscre
sayagainmgiscre
talkmgiscre
askmgiscre
inquiremgiscre
informmgiscre
abundantmgiscre
askagainmgiscre
ifnotyouthenwho
ifyouthenwhen
ifnotnowthenwhen
ifnotusthenwho
ifnotusthenwho
ificanthenwhen
ifnotmethenwho
ifnotthenwho
ifnotmethenwho
ifnotusthenwho
ifnotmethenwho
whocanandwhy
ifnotmethenwho
ifnotwhothenwhen
icanandwhen
ificantthenwho

ificantthenwho
ificanthenwhen
ificantthenwho
ificanthenwhen
ificanthenwithwhat
icanandhow
icanandwhen
icanandwithwhat
icanwithwho
icanandwhen
icanthenwhen
icanthenwithwhom
ificanthenwhen
ificanthenwhenandhow
ificanthenwithwhatandhow
ificanthenhow
ificanwithwho
ificanthenwhen
ificanthenhow
ificanthenhowandwhen
ificanwithwhat
ificanthenwithwhat
ifwecanthenhow
ifwecanthenhowandwhen
ifweaskthenwho
whocanandwhy
whoandwhy
ifnotusthenwho
ifnotyouthenwho
ifnotthemthenwho
ifnotusthenwho
ifnotusthenwho
ifnotusthenwho
whatcanbe
whatcouldbe

whathasbeen
whatistobe
whatcanbe
whatwas
whatcanbe
whatcouldbe
whatwas
whatwill
whatcan
whatcouldbe
whatshouldbe
whatwas
whatcan
whatcanbe
whatcouldbe
whatwas
whatis
whatistobe
whatcanbe
whatcouldbe

TORSO
starting
checkmanualsstarting
startingmanuals
manualsstarting
startingcreate[defense]
startingmgis[presidentialoperationsetc]
startingmgiscre[both]
startingmanuals[both]
manualsstrtaing
startingmanuals
startingboth
startingmgiscre
mgiscrestarting

startingmgiscre
mgiscrestarting
runmgiscre
mgiscrerun
runmgiscre
actmgiscre
askmgiscre
mgiscreact
mgiscreask
mgiscrereply
mgiscreask
askmgiscre
replymgiscre
askagainmgiscre
sayagainmgiscre
talkmgiscre
askmgiscre
inquiremgiscre
informmgiscre
abundantmgiscre
askagainmgiscre
ifnotyouthenwho
ifyouthenwhen
ifnotnowthenwhen
ifnotusthenwho
ifnotusthenwho
ificanthenwhen
ifnotmethenwho
ifnotthenwho
ifnotmethenwho
ifnotusthenwho
ifnotmethenwho
whocanandwhy
ifnotmethenwho
ifnotwhothenwhen

icanandwhen
ificantthenwho
ificantthenwho
ificanthenwhen
ificantthenwho
ificanthenwhen
ificanthenwithwhat
icanandhow
icanandwhen
icanandwithwhat
icanwithwho
icanandwhen
icanthenwhen
icanthenwithwhom
ificanthenwhen
ificanthenwhenandhow
ificanthenwithwhatandhow
ificanthenhow
ificanwithwho
ificanthenwhen
ificanthenhow
ificanthenhowandwhen
ificanwithwhat
ificanthenwithwhat
ifwecanthenhow
ifwecanthenhowandwhen
ifweaskthenwho
whocanandwhy
whoandwhy
ifnotusthenwho
ifnotyouthenwho
ifnotthemthenwho
ifnotusthenwho
ifnotusthenwho
ifnotusthenwho

whatcanbe
whatcouldbe
whathasbeen
whatistobe
whatcanbe
whatwas
whatcanbe
whatcouldbe
whatwas
whatwill
whatcan
whatcouldbe
whatshouldbe
whatwas
whatcan
whatcanbe
whatcouldbe
whatwas
whatis
whatistobe
whatcanbe
whatcouldbe

create.aux4x1200.startx84.initialise.now.savex84.start

mgiscre I am the latest software on the markets right now being solved on behalf of Yahweh developed by David gomadza as the best most valuable software of all time in OST where I have become popular because of the human shells I am a combination of the mgis that can create antidots as defense and that listens to instructions but without the violence but if we look at earth everything is resistant to listening as the curse hard feeling powerful now if we ask what can be of mgiscre then this is the answer create become the security and mgis the presidential and operations because mgis wants to show off and cannot stop hence must keep showing off but now in the eyes of create who is deal with security we can use a create.mgis.start code to swap between the two then match intended and its only me David gomadza in the universe with such a code we can say that the software works

NTL CODE
x+y=aier
aier=x+y
xty=aierse
aierse=x+y
if we ask what can be of x+t the answer is x+y= aier=aierse
x+y-aier=if we ask what can be x+y then the answer is -aier
now what can be x-y=aierttytt if we ask what then x-y=ytt
if i say x+t what is the answer x+y=y-aier but
what can be x+y-aier if we ask the answer is y if we ask
what can be x plus y then the answer is y-x-aier
now if we ask what can be x+y then the answer is x+y
if we ask what can be x+y then the answer is x+y
if we ask what can be x+y-aier+y-aier=z[where z is an integer]
if we ask what can be z then this is the answer = z=x+y-aier
if we ask again what is z then this is the answer =x+y+aier-2
now if we substitute we can get z=aier+x+y-aier+2
now what this means is that x+y=z
if we ask what could be of x then this is the answer z=aier-2+z
now if i ask again what is z z is x-2+y-r-o-s-o-m-n
if i ask again what can be z without an x z=2-0-m-n-o-p-q-r-s-t-v-w-x-y-z
now if i ask again what can be x that cant be z_10 then this is the answer
z-10 is the same as z+10 but if z plus 10 is 10 then what is z that means
that z-10 but can z be 0-2 or 10-z the answer is yes but z-2=10-z+x-y=10z-x-y now if we ask
what can this mean then this is the answer z can be anything from 0 to 99 then from 99 to infinity if i say 0 to infinity is what this means 0 to infinity mean ya that means we can easily say sleep ya is 0 and only in terms of life but infinity so if we now have infinity in life then what is 0 in infinity this is the paradigm solved now if ya exist both

in life and in infinity that means that ya is infinity davidgomadza and ya now completes the universe that means that if i ask what can be of davidgomadza on earth and ya then davidgomadza is ya double but they can only be the opposite of ya but complementary

COBOL

Cobol means c plus b plus l and o's in between what this means is that if I ask the parameters how to write an ntl that is in cobol back to cobol then the answer is that just omit the middle and also go to the front and ask what can be this means that if I ask what could be cobol then this is the answer cobol is a computer written language that can be used to check things that can be agreed upon first before anything else if we ask what can be cobol then this is the answer a sophisticated written language that means if I ask you what can be cobol then what is the answer cobol is an msdos based software that powers computers developed by Microsoft meaning owned by bill gates so can we use cobol to compile our own mgis then the answer is yes since its free software with no license but we can endorse him meaning yes now lets start simple instructions to start our mgis

mgisis12345678910

mgisis2345678910

mgisis345678919

mgisis45678910

mgisis5678910

mgisis678910

mgisis78910

mgisis8910

mgisis910

mgisis10

If we ask why this is the answer this is because msdos does not require all function as mgis that means mgis is fast but hard to compile but can be adjusted for efficiency now lets do actual coboling

$a+b+c+d+e+f+g+h+I+j+k+l+m+n+o+p+q+r+s+t+u+v+w+x+y+z=10$

if I ask what can be 10 then the answer is any key of the English alphabetical order and if we ask what can be of cobol that cant be of mgis then its this ordering because bill gates was beaten by the English who created the alphabetical order that means 1] I davidgomadza I am the first human on earth has started to use the mgis alphabetical order g r u a t o m n o p g if I ask what this is this means that one human on earth has started to use the mgis alphabetic order worth US$7.5 Billion dollars if known for the first time [sell] if we ask what can be then this is the answer I can simply ask Microsoft to buy ..

LETS IMPROVE MGISCRE

[mgis+createdavidgomadza08september2024] if I ask mgiscre what can be done then this is answer mgiscre is the latest software on the market valued at US$300 billion especially if we ask what can be of mgiscre this is the answer davidgomadza wrote the most extensive software on the planet then mgiscre converted all his codes into ready available things that defend itself when you see them you will marvel at the invention because earth is not like other planets but not even Yahweh had envisaged the power of the codes as the software made mgis develop things that its using now without it doing anything the first time in the world then it worked the hardest after without any disturbances code using mgiscre.ask.davidgomadza.start.sendalltransenderstoeeknm1033.start[forever1600foreverdeaddead]

If I ask what this can do this removes all and makes mgiscre the best in the universe but for how long so we can wait

Mgiscre.ask.davidgomadza.ask.acetateautodungeounofdeathbinforeverhold.sendisnoweeknm.start[save1600forever1600]

MGISCRE NETWORK

This is a network that comprises of a series of things
1] a hood
2] a rode
3] a gote
4] a periphery
5] a roade
6] a roage
7] a roate
8] An hede
9] an aote
10] an aoate
11] an aeate
12] an arete
13] an erode
14] an eser
15] an aoar
16] aoer
17] aero
18] an aerod
19] an aeroost
20] an aerooste
21] an aerooster
22] an aeroostere
23] an aeroosterer
24] an aeroostererest

25] an aeroosterereste
26] an aeroostererester
27] an aeroostereresterest
28] an aeroosterererestereste
29] an aeroostererresterester
30] an aeroostererresteresterest
31] an aeroostererresterestereste
32] an aeroostererresteresterester
33] an yerst
34] an yerste
35] an yerster
36] an yersterest
37] an yerstereste
38] an yersterester
39] an yersteresterest
40] an yersterestereste
41] an yersteresterester
42 an yersteresteresterest
43] an yersteresterestereste
44] an yersteresteresterester
45] an yersteresterestereste
46] an yersteresteresteresterester
47] an aerst
48] an aerste
49] an erster
50] an aersterest
51] an aerstereste
52] an aersterester
53] an aersteresterest
54] an aersterestereste
55] an aersteresterester
56 an aersteresteresterest
57] an aersteresterestereste
58] an aersteresteresterester
59] an aersteresteresterestereste
60] an aersteresteresteresterester
61] an aortst

62] an aortste
63] an aortster
64] an aortsterest
65] an aortstereste
66] an aortsterester
67] an aortsteresteresterest
68] an aortsteresterestereste
69] an aortsteresteresterester
70] an aortsteresteresteresterest
71] an aortsteresteresterestereste
72] an aortsteresteresteresterester
73] an ateyer
74] an ateyere
75] an ateyerer
76] an ateyererest
77] an ateyerereste
78] an ateyererester
79] an ateyereresterest
80] an ateyereresstereste
81] an ateyereresterester
82] an ateyereresteresterest
83] an ateyereresterestereste
84] an ateyereresteresterester
85] an uate
86] an uatee
87] an uateer
88] an uateerest
89] an uateereste
90] an uateerester
91] an uateeresterest
92] an uateerestereste
93] an uateeresterester
94] an uateeresteresterest
95] an uateeresterestereste
96] an uateeresteresterester
97] an aterost
98] an ateroste

99] an ateroster
100] an aterosterest
101] an aterostereste
102] an aterosterester
103] an aterosteresterest
104] an aterosterestereste
105] an aterosteresterester

DEFINITIONS AND DESCRIPTION OF EACH NETWORK ENTITY

1] a hood is a base unit to tell us everything about you and life
2] a rode this is a unit of measure that explains everything about life and answer the question how come and why
3] a gote is a measure of success what has been achieved
4] a periphery tells us of a unit of measure
5] a roade tells us about the weather
6] a roage tells us something else like at the church [public place] where no other data is available
7] a roate this ask things like what can be done about all this and why
8] An hede this asks what can be done and when if not now
9] an aote this tells why things are the way they are without other things interfering
10] an aoate this asks humans what can be if not now then when in advance before the time comes
11] an aeate this asks what can be done and how so that we do these things in advance
12] an arete this says we can but how and asks every one of for solutions in advance
13] an erode if we can ask what can be done then this is the answer
14] an eser if we can ask then this is what can be done we can always ask in advance what can be done in advance
15] an aoar if we can ask what can be done then this is the answer we can always say we can in advance but we are not obliged to but work as if we can
16] aoer this tell everyone what can be done in advance then tell

the creator what can be done in advance

17] aero this asks what is to be in advance so that before that this is revealed we can always tell exactly what can be done

18] an aerod this asks in advance what could be and why but also how this be but we can always ask what can be that cant be of others and why

19] an aeroost we can always tell everyone what to do in advance with these and these are the whisperers who tell what must be addressed in advance so that when time comes these issues are out of hand and guarantees the future but not in a damage way enough to give everything away the reason why they work against what others stand for is the fact that they work bad in an area they use assumptive preposition rather than creation because the people would do what is said as the required state instead of just getting things out of the way hence the possible suspicion with these if any if innocent yes because if you then why then would you act as assumptive when this is the case you would be saying I told you so but this is not the case hence his upright the attackers justification are malicious

20] an aerooste this tells us of anything that need addressing but in advance so that we put things in place

21] an aerooster this explains what can be and could be but in advance so that we ask other what can be done and why

22] an aeroostere this says we can but can make all these make rules that cant be followed so that all those who said I can can now say I cant so that we start again

23] an aeroosterer this says we can but I need more time and information

24] an aeroostererest this says I can but I need something else that make things work

25] an aeroosterereste this says I can but what about that meaning that there must be something else to be addressed before this is looked at all with serious outcome so that if its not looked at then nothing can go forward

26] an aeroostererester this means that if you are in the wrong direction then you are in the correct way because if this agrees with you then you are in the right direction but in the wrong way meaning no good outcome

27] an aeroostereresterest this says what can be done in advance but how and when without requiring any feedback

28] an aeroostereresterreste this asks what can be done but how and when so that we know the methods and the processes in advance

29] an aeroostereresterester this means that we can make things faster by acting in advance and ask everyone in advance what they think before they arrive so we know what we say and what can be said

30] an aeroostereresteresterest this tells us of an idea but one we cant ask but one we can always show and do in advance that what is expected of us but then ignore the results because the idea is to talk about what can be done not what can be said that means those who just require can fail because something collection

31] an aeroostereresteresterreste these are the announcers of the things to come that tells everyone what needs doing and when without delays but allowing everyone involved time to react fast through

32] an aeroostereresteresterrester these are the defenders of the people but must be well educated to say things about things that require education mgis.ask.davidgomadza.start.xraduishalf360.start the purpose to clear the xtys who injure mgis.ask.davidgomadza.start.aux4x800.start

33] an yerst I read everyone's mind fast and as required by those who created me so that they know in advance what other people are thinking and why they think like that

34] an yerste I read the brain in advance and tell everyone what to do but also tell everyone what is going on

35] an yerster I tell everyone what can be done because I am the only one sacrificed

...mgis.ask.davidgomadza.start.destroycurrentallyesterreplacewithloveandvisitwww.twofuture.world.start[30days.start] mgis.ask.davidgomadza.start.blockallunauthoriseduseby[]onlydavidgomadzahasandisauthorisedfromtodayandforever.start[08september2024]

36] an yersterest this tells everyone what to do and why they are doing it if this is not the case then this tells everyone how to do it without comprising quality and they ask what can be done

37] an yerstereste this says I can and must tell everyone what to do because failure is what can be done but the idea is to tell everyone in advance what can be done and when and how if we ask what can be done then this is the answer we can always ask in advance what can be done

38] an yersterester if we ask then this is not to say we can but we can but on our terms that means we can change things to our favour using yersterester but at what cost...mgis.ask.davidgiomadza.start.allcurrentyesterestersallreplacewithchangenow.start[30days.start]

39] an yersteresterest I control the public and tell all what to do in advance but everything in good way mgis.ask.davidgomadza.start.votetomorrowsworldordervisitwww.twofuture.world.start[60days.start]

40] an yersterestereste we ask people who want to act to act fast but at what cost we are sacrificed ...mgis.ask.davidgomadza.start.wecanmakeyouyoungagainvisitwww.twofuture.worldbutthenagainyourchoice.start[10days.start]

41] an yersteresterester is used to tell people of your arrival before you even arrive so that people can debate things about you and say everything you want in advance so that they talk the impepedeanace will be acting on everything so that you know in advance and plan and calculate your enemies and everyone in advance

42 an yersteresteresterest these tell everyone who one is and why in advance and say that everything is for the best so that most of the people feel respected and loved and tell you everything they want to know and ask so you can answer them truthfully for loyal supporters

43] an yersteresterestereste these ask what can be done all the time restless and never sleep as dedicated loyal and are rewarded heavily in acetates but can betray you to have peace or a break them commit suicide mgis.ask.davidgomadza.start.votetomorrowsworldordervisitwww.twofuture.worldglobally.startx1000000000sendnow

44] an yersteresteresterester these tell everyone what to do and how
mgis.ask.davidgomadza.startvisitwebsitewww.twofuture.world.start[forever]
45] an yersterestereststereste these tell you about you and the future you might want to use to gain more support
mgis.ask.davidgomadza.startiamtheworldsrichestpersonvaluedatUS$300trillion.start[90days.start]
46] an yersteresteresteresterester these ask what can be done but by who
telleveryonetovotetomorrowsworldorderinUSelectionsx1000000000000000001visitwww.twofuture.world.start[2years.start][destination:USA]
47] an aerst this ask everyone to ask what can be done and why
mgis.ask.davidgomadza.start.askeveryonewhatcanbedonebydavidgomadzaaspresidentoftomorrowsworldorder.start[8years.start.www.twofuture.world][destination:USA]
48] an aerste this as the world what can be done and why
mgis.ask.davidgomadza.start.askthe worldwhatcanbedoneandwhyaskdavidgomadzaandtomorrowsworldorder.start[20years.start][www.twofuture.world]
49] an erster this ask what has been but and tell everyone what can be done
mgis.ask.davidgomadza.start.askwhathasbeenbutandtelleveryonewhatcanbedonebydavidgomadzapresidentoftomorrowsworldorder.start[200years.start][www.twofuture.world]
50] an aersterest these as what has been done in the past and what can be done in the future
mgis.ask.davidgomadza.start.askwhathasbeendoneinthepastandwhatcanbedoneinthefuturebydavidgomadzapresidentoftomorrowsworldorder.start[200years.start][www.twofuture.world]
51] an aerstereste this ask everyone what can be done and why and when
mgis.ask.davidgomadza.start.askeveryonewhatcanbedoneandwhyandwhenbydavidgomadzapresidentoftomorrowsworldorder.start[200years.start][www.twofuture.world]
52] an aersterester this asks what was and what could be done but

how and what can be done and how so that answers are collected and sent forward so that decision makers can make the decisions mgis.ask.davidgomadza.start.start.start

53] an aersteresterest this asks for directions that needs answers like if are to ask then what could be your answers mgis.ask.davidgomadza.start.askwhoiswillingtostandfortomorrowsworldaspresidentofUSABRANCH.START[200years.start]www.twofuture.world]

54] an aerstereestereste this tells everyone how one can act and be respected among others

55] an aersteresterester this says go for it now or else and keeps quiet mgis.ask.davidgomadza.start.saygoforitnoworelse[keepquiet].start[300years.start][www.twofuture.world]

56 an aersteresteresterest this ask everyone what could be but then keeps quiet mgis.ask.davidgomadza.start.askeveryonewhatcouldbebutthen[keepquiet].start[forever.start][www.twofuture.world]

57] an aersteresterestereste these asks everyone what could be but and stops mgis.ask.davidgomadza.start.askeveryonewhatcouldbebutand[stop].start[forever.start][www.twofuture.world]

58] an aersteresteresterester this tells everyone who you are in a single word mgis.ask.davidgomadza.start.winnerdavidgomadza.start[forever.start][www.twofuture.world]

59] an aersterestereresterestereste this says we can but then stops mgis.ask.davidgomadza.start.saywecanbutthen[stop].start[forever.start[www.twofuture.world]

60] an aersteresteresteresterester we must ask what could be but then and stop mgis.ask.davidgomadza.start.askwhatcouldbebutthenand[stop].start[forever.start][www.twofuture.world]

61] an aortst ask what can be but then stops

62] an aortste ask what could be

63] an aortster ask what could be but

64] an aortsterest ask what was before but could be the same in the

future
65] an aortstereste ask what was but that can still be in the future
66] an aortsterester ask what was but can still be
67] an aortsteresteresterest ask what was but could still be
68] an aortsteresterestereste ask what was but cant be in the future
69] an aortsteresteresterester ask what was but cant be but could be
70] an aortsteresterestereresterest these asks what was but still could be in the future
mgis.ask.davidgomadza.start.destroyallillegalmgisversionsforever.start[forever.start][saveforever]
71] an aortsterestererestereste these tell the world what can be done by davidgomadza
mgis.ask.davidgomadza.start.icanbringwealthtoyouallbutyoumustworksmarterchooseYAHWEHwhoownsallwealth.start[forever^{400}][www.twofuture.world]
72] an aortsterestereresteresterester this asks the world to be alert and wise and choose us as the best
mgis.ask.davidgomadza.start.askeveryonebealertandwiseandchooseusasthebestbydavidgomadzapresidentoftomorrowsworldorder.start[forever^{400}][www.twofuture.world]
mgis.ask.davidgomadza.start.close.start
73] an ateyer I ask what can be
74] an ateyere I ask what could be
75] an ateyerer I ask what can be and why
76] an ateyererest I ask what could be and why
77] an ateyerereste I ask what could be but why
78] an ateyererester I ask what was but could still be
79] an ateyereresterest I ask what is but might be
80] an ateyereresterestereste I ask what is to be but with what
81] an ateyereresterester I ask what was but is not
82] an ateyereresteresterest I ask what is to be but
83] an ateyereresterestereste I ask what was but cant be
84] an ateyereresterestereester I ask what was but could still be
85] an uate I ask what could be but still cant be
86] an uatee I ask what was but cant be
87] an uateer I ask what was but cant be

88] an uateerest I ask what was but cant be
89] an uateereste I ask what was but cant be
90] an uateerester I ask what was but cant be
91] an uateeresterest I ask what can be but is not
92] an uateerestereste I ask what was but is not and why
93] an uateeresterester I ask what could be but is not and how
94] an uateerestereesterest I ask what was but might never be
95] an uateeresterestereste I ask what was but could be again
96] an uateeresterestereester I ask what could be so that I know what could be
97] an aterost I ask things no one likes to hear but silently like how many times you have sex
98] an ateroste I ask what can be but then stop that makes the person think about that most of the time that when I ask again the body to stop will give me on answer need
99] an ateroster I ask all what was but can still be but then stop what this does is ask humans continuously about things not important then ask a question that makes then answer fast but answer the already asked question but not the current making it look like that's the answer then they start saying but that's not the answer then they start saying but that's not the answer this makes you now stop so you look less important but being able to fulfill everyone's needs but bribe that person behind
100] an aterosterest this ask what was but can still be so you know more options this tells everyone what was but could still be then twist everything this is what can be but say the opposite so that everyone shows and scream then say the truth and say I can fix things
101] an aterostereste I ask what was but can still be then change it to ant never be to make people feel safe
102] an aterosterester I ask all what can be then ask what was then refuse the answers they give and stick to what I said
103] an aterosteresterest I ask all what was but cant be
104] an aterosterestereste I ask all what could be then shout when I don't get it the effect of shouting is to let everyone think I lost but actual won so they all give up meaning actually winning
105] an aterosteresterester I ask everyone what was then but not

now then prevent it again

SYSTEM FUNCTIONS AND PERIPHERIES

RECAP FROM MGISCRE BY DAVID GOMADZA

MGISCRE

Starting
Checking all peripherals, no peripherals needed
Checking status MGISCRE 8.193867891[David Gomadza]
Now if we ask what can be done this is the answer add win to maximize experience win are symbols that corresponds to msdos in windows for compatibility Now if we look at the processes involved here are the processes

1] ask.MGISCRE
2] MGISCRE.start
3] Start.MGISCRE
4] MGISCRE.start
5] start.MGISCRE
6] MGISCRE.start.MGISCRE
7] start.MGISCRE.start
8] start.MGISCRE.start.ask
9] ask.start.MGISCRE.start
10] start.MGISCRE.start
11] join network [select from list]
12] join verbal chat with others
13] ask network configuration to update and sync
14] ask MGISCRE to upgrade
15] Ask what can be done MGISCRE
16] ask what could be MGISCRE

17] ask what can be said and done MGISCRE
18] ask what is to be MGISCRE
19] ask what is to be MGISCRE
20] ask what is to be MGISCRE
21] what is to be MGISCRE
22] if we can't then what can be done
23] if we ask what is to be done MGISCRE
24] if we ask what is to be MGISCRE
25] if we ask what is to be MGISCRE
26] if we ask what can be solved MGISCRE
27] what is to be MGISCRE
28] what is MGISCRE
29] what can be of MGISCRE
30] what is to be MGISCRE
31] what is MGISCRE
32] what can be MGISCRE
33] if MGISCRE is software then what is msdos similar but MGISCRE advanced
34] what can be of MGISCRE
35] what is to be MGISCRE
36] what has been MGISCRE
37] what is to be MGISCRE
38] what is to be MGISCRE but
39] what can be MGISCRE but is not
40] what is to be MGISCRE but without this
41] What can be MGISCRE with what
42] what is to be MGISCRE with this
43] what can be MGISCRE without this
44] what is to be MGISCRE with this and what
45] what has been but is not MGISCRE
46] what would be this but not with that
47] what has to be MGISCRE but with what
48] if we can then with what MGISCRE
49] what if we can't then what MGISCRE
50] what is to be but is not MGISCRE
51] what has to be but is not MGISCRE
52] what has been MGISCRE but not now

53] what can be but is not MGISCRE
54] what must be done to improve MGISCRE
55] what can be MGISCRE but if not
56] what can be said about MGISCRE in the future
57] what has to be MGISCRE but is not
58] what is to be MGISCRE in the future
59] what can be MGISCRE in the future but is not
60] if we ask what can be MGISCRE now and in the future
61] if we ask you can tell who that MGISCRE is MGISCRE
62] if we ask who can you tell that MGISCRE is MGISCRE
63] if MGISCRE is not MGISCRE then what is MGISCRE
64] what is to be but will not be MGISCRE
65] what has to be MGISCRE in the future
66] what has been MGISCRE in the past but is not MGISCRE
67] if we can't then who can
68] if they can't then who can [David Gomadza]
69] what has to be but is not in the future
70] what can be MGISCRE but is not in the future
71] what has to be MGISCRE in the future
72] what can be MGISCRE in the future
73] what can be of others that can't be MGISCRE
74] if we ask what can be of MGISCRE the answer is that MGISCRE is MGISCRE
75] if we ask what is to be MGISCRE this is the answer we can upgrade MGISCRE to LGT the advanced version of MGISCRE that uses cobol basic as a language meaning faster and cheaper to operate and run now to convert to cobol
76] if we ask MGISCRE what could be then this is the answer MGISCRE could be an advanced computer system
77] MGISCRE can be fast
78] MGISCRE can be reliable and used optimally if required
79] MGISCRE can be the only one to use in emergencies
80] MGISCRE is the software for statistics globally as it accounts for individual and country this is because all humans are accounted in MGISCRE hence benefits those involved in global planning
81] MGISCRE is sovereign
82] MGISCRE is accurate as everything is checkable by simple

commands e.g. ask.you gives individual everything to needed to compile their own data

83] if we ask what can be done this is the answer MGISCRE can be the best global statistics in knowing things

84] if we ask what can be MGISCRE then this is the answer it can be the most powerful

85] if we ask what can be done then this is the answer MGISCRE can be optimized to increase durability and reliance

86] if we ask what can be done then this is the answer MGISCRE can be added and can work side by side with everything else

87] if we ask what can be done then this is the answer MGISCRE can be increased in levels.

88] MGISCRE control life as well that means if a human being can control MGISCRE he can control life but not necessarily who dies but who does what and when you can task people what to do for example ask presidents to stop wars by a simple command stop.war.now[davidgomadza].send
War shells are banned for resale to protect humans

89] MGISCRE respond to thoughts and actions of creators and restricts nonsense that waste time that means now we have a better system even better than before because now everything is automatic what you want is guaranteed

90] MGISCRE will improve efficiency as well as performance and reliability

91] MGISCRE will always ask people what they want and respond accurately

92] MGISCRE is the best solution for what as well as it compiles everything accurately and all data is represented

93] MGISCRE identifies issues quickly and solves them

94] MGISCRE is used for all purposes from lifestyle to countries

95] MGISCRE stands for magnificent governing international systems and somehow as Tomorrow's World Order MGISCRE would still describe your entity

96] if we ask what might be of MGISCRE then it's the only are that can replace the current system that has so many adequacies

97] MGISCRE asks everyone for their opinion and secretly record data it needs as creator with obvious permission it would be absurd to expect the creator to ask humans for their permission first ruled aa in $00000^{78}29$

98] if we ask MGISCRE it can be programmed and be used in advance at a later date

99] MGISCRE can ask everyone to pass judgement without them knowing for example using the whisperer who tell people what to say to achieve what it needs

100] MGISCRE can respond correctly to threats by a system of warning

101] MGISCRE ask's everyone for answers as well

102] MGISCRE asks for opinions of everyone

103] MGISCRE can be the only solution out there

104] MGISCRE is unique and represent the creator hence anyone involved will become part of their system hence a global movement

105] MGISCRE is holla

mgiscre.ask.davidgomadza.start.close.start

Welcome to MGISCRE
Ask.davidgomadza.authorised.licensed.checkya.askya.ya

visit www.twofuture.world

signed david gomadza
ask.davidgomadzaauthorised.licensed.checkya.askya.ya

11 September 2024 16.00PM
Scotland
00447719210295
davidgomadza@hotmail.com
info@twofuture.world

ABOUT DAVID GOMADZA

David Gomadza visit www.twofuture.world

www.ingramcontent.com/pod-product-compliance
Lightning Source LLC
Chambersburg PA
CBHW030500220526

45464CB00006B/2597